>>CHEER
TRYOUTS
AND TRAINING

BY MARCIA AMIDON LUSTED

CONTENT CONSULTANT

Pauline Zernott
Spirit Director and Coach
Louisiana State University

SportsZone
An Imprint of Abdo Publishing | abdopublishing.com

ABDOPUBLISHING.COM

Published by Abdo Publishing, a division of ABDO, PO Box 398166, Minneapolis, Minnesota 55439. Copyright © 2016 by Abdo Consulting Group, Inc. International copyrights reserved in all countries. No part of this book may be reproduced in any form without written permission from the publisher. SportsZone™ is a trademark and logo of Abdo Publishing.

Printed in the United States of America, North Mankato, Minnesota
082015
012016

THIS BOOK CONTAINS
RECYCLED MATERIALS

Cover Photo: Shutterstock Images
Interior Photos: Shutterstock Images, 4–5, 7, 12, 14–15, 29; Digital Vision/Photodisc/Thinkstock, 6; Reza A. Marvashti/The Free Lance–Star/AP Images, 8–9; iStock/Thinkstock, 10; Stockbyte/Thinkstock, 13; Louis-Paul St-Onge/iStockphoto, 16; Fuse/Thinkstock, 17 (top); Julio Cortez/AP Images, 17 (bottom), 18–19; iStockphoto, 20–21; Chris Matula/ZumaPress/Newscom, 22; Mike Watson Images/Moodboard/Thinkstock, 24–25; Richard Thornton/Shutterstock Images, 26; Cherie Diez/ZumaPress/Newscom, 28

Editor: Mirella Miller
Series Designer: Maggie Villaume

Library of Congress Control Number: 2015945769

Cataloging-in-Publication Data
Lusted, Marcia Amidon.
 Cheer tryouts and training / Marcia Amidon Lusted.
  p. cm. -- (Cheerleading)
ISBN 978-1-62403-984-3 (lib. bdg.)
Includes bibliographical references and index.
1. Cheerleading--Juvenile literature.   I. Title.
791.6/4--dc23

                                                        2015945769

CONTENTS

ONE

BECOMING A CHEERLEADER

Being a cheerleader can be exciting. First you must try out to join a school team or other cheer squad. This means performing for the coach or other cheerleaders. The coaches decide who will be the best new cheerleaders. They pick who will join the team.

Find out about cheerleading before going to tryouts. Go to some cheerleading practices, and watch what the team does. Talk to cheerleaders already on the squad. Will you need to perform a routine that you have already practiced? What is expected from cheerleaders on the team? How many practices, training sessions, and games do they attend?

The cheerleaders who do the best at tryouts join the squad.

Older cheerleaders may go to tryouts to cheer on the new cheerleaders.

GO TEAMS!

Cheerleaders may be part of a school's sports team. There are also cheerleading teams that are not part of specific schools. They compete in contests. There are different levels of cheerleading at most schools. Junior varsity cheerleaders cheer for the sports teams made up of younger students. Varsity cheerleaders cheer for the teams made up of older students who have more experience and skill.

It may sound scary having to try out in front of a group of people. If you are prepared and practice ahead of time, you can do your very best. Tryouts can be difficult. They can also be fun. Being prepared makes it much easier.

Working hard and practicing cheer skills before tryouts is helpful.

TWO
GETTING READY

It is important to start getting ready for tryouts long before they happen. Cheerleaders need to be in good shape. They must be able to flip, lift, and jump. If you are not ready, you might have sore muscles at tryouts.

Exercise is always important. It is even more necessary for anyone who wants to be a cheerleader. Sports such as gymnastics and activities such as yoga help with flexibility and stamina. Stretching before any physical activity helps prevent soreness and injuries.

Practicing gymnastics can help cheerleaders with their skills.

Being creative
with your routine
shows leadership
and preparation.

It is also important to eat the right food. Try to avoid junk food and energy drinks. They provide a short burst of energy. But soon after, your energy level can crash. Also make sure to get plenty of sleep before tryout day. All these things are good practices to continue once you make the cheerleading team.

At some tryouts, coaches teach a simple routine and have people perform it after they learn it. At other tryouts, cheerleaders must come prepared with their own routines. Learn a routine the team has done in the past. Or maybe practice and perform a routine from another cheer team. With an adult's help, find cheerleading routines on the Internet. Get ideas from the videos you watch.

Practice the arm movements that go with each chant.

It is helpful to practice not only the physical moves for cheering but the vocal part as well. Learning cheer chants and practicing them out loud makes it easier on tryout day. Learn chants the cheer team already uses. It is a good idea to learn a few new chants too. Watch other cheer teams or watch Internet videos for ideas. Knowing the chants and being able to yell them clearly and loudly is an important part of cheering.

Finally remember that attitude plays a huge role in tryouts. Try to be confident and calm. It is easier to do well if you already have a winning attitude.

Smile big and have fun during tryouts.

THREE

TRYOUT
DAY

It is tryout day. It is natural to be nervous. Eat a healthy breakfast with foods that provide energy. These include protein, such as eggs, milk, cheese, soy, and yogurt. Grains such as whole wheat bread or granola also help keep energy levels high. Bodies do not work well without nutrition. Wear comfortable clothes that are easy to move in, such as shorts or tight pants and a T-shirt.

It is important to be friendly and to interact with other cheerleaders at tryouts. Being nice and supportive shows teamwork. Talking to others also makes it easier when other people are feeling nervous. It is a good idea to show the judges that you work well with other people.

Other people at tryouts may become future teammates and friends.

TRYOUT TIPS

Be sure to warm up with the group or alone. It is important not to do anything that might injure you or that you are not comfortable with. At some tryouts, you will perform as a group. Other times you might perform the routine one at a time. Usually the coach and other team members are watching.

Stretch your muscles and practice any moves you are nervous about.

Even professional cheerleaders must go through tryouts.

You might learn a cheer routine from the coach or experienced cheerleaders.

No matter what routine is being done, attitude is important. Being cheerful and excited shows the judges you will have the same attitude on the cheer team. Cheerleading is performing. Performers need to look happy and make the audience feel happy too. Acting confident, even when you have made a mistake, also makes a good impression.

After the tryouts are done, the judges score the performance and talk among themselves. They may announce who made the team that day. Or they might think about it and post the results later.

ATTITUDE

It is normal after a tryout to focus on what went wrong. Even a major mess-up is nothing to be upset over. Chances are it was not as obvious to the judges as it was to you. It will also help you be more prepared next time.

Putting on a good performance during tryouts will help the coaches remember you when it is time to choose the team.

FOUR

MAKING THE TEAM

The results are posted. The newest members of the cheerleading team have been chosen. Your name is there! You are now a cheerleader. What happens next?

The cheerleading coach will hand out a schedule of practices and games. It is important to treat this schedule seriously and to show up for all events. Being a cheerleader is a commitment.

The coach or equipment manager will pass out uniforms to new members. They will also provide any rules about shoes, jewelry, and hairstyles. The team might also give out props such as pom-poms or batons.

The coach will give instructions on how to take care of your uniform.

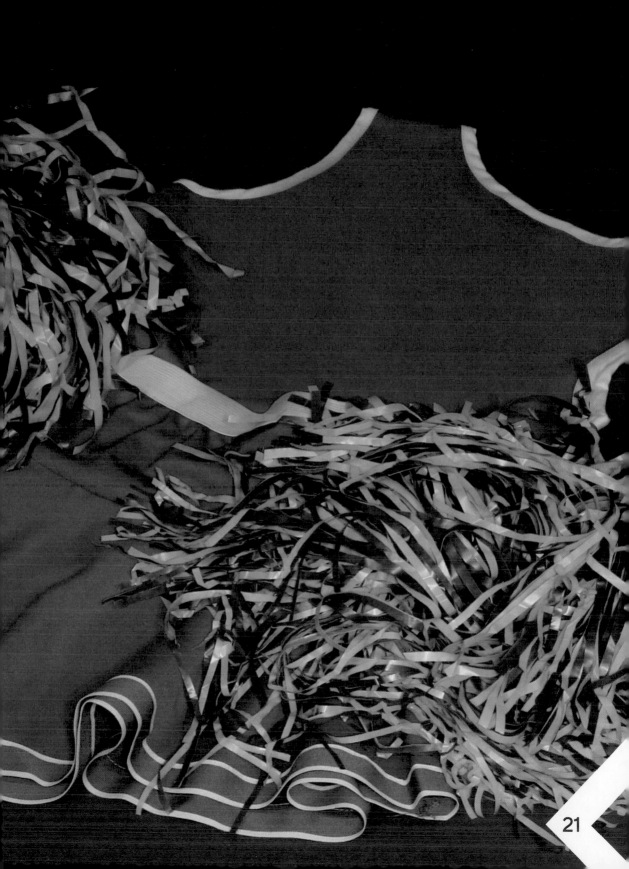

The first cheerleading practice might include getting to know your teammates. Rules, schedules, and travel are explained. Some teams must ride on a team bus for events. Once all of this is done, the real practicing begins.

At most practices, there will be a warm-up, followed by learning routines and cheers. The cheerleaders focus on learning and perfecting routines. New members with less experience do easier stunts and jumps. They are taught more complicated moves as they learn and get better. Practice is also about teamwork. Cheerleaders must work together to make their routines perfect.

Training with weights, taking gymnastics or dance lessons, building strength, and stretching are ways to stay in top condition. Eating well, sleeping enough, and drinking plenty of water are also things you should always do.

Cheerleaders exercise and train outside of school too.

FIVE

CLINICS
AND CAMPS

The cheerleading coach and other cheer team members teach most skills needed for cheerleading. Some schools might bring in experts for special training or workshops. There are also many online resources for new ideas for routines and chants. Videos show stunts and other moves. However, it is important not to try a stunt or jump, especially a difficult one, after seeing it on video. Many stunts require spotters who are there to support and catch team members during stunts. Doing them alone and without proper teaching can be dangerous.

Do not try any new stunts without practicing them first.

A group of girls practice a routine at a summer cheerleading camp.

There are other ways to grow your skills as a cheerleader. Many training programs are available outside of school. These can be one-day clinics or regular classes. A guest coach from another school or from a college might lead them.

PRIVATE COACHING

There are many professional training programs for cheerleaders. Many of these are for girls who want to cheer for professional sports teams. These programs can be special cheerleading schools with a series of weekly training classes. There are also private coaches who work one-on-one with cheerleaders.

There are also special summer camps for cheerleaders. These camps bring together cheerleading experts who teach new skills and routines, with regular camp activities, recreation, and fitness. Camps can be a great way to meet and talk to other cheerleaders. Making friends and sharing information is as important as learning new skills.

Camps are good places to learn and practice new skills.

Any extra outside training can be a great way to learn new cheers, routines, jumps, and stunts. It can also be helpful to attend other schools' sporting events and see what their cheerleaders are doing.

Going to tryouts is a good first step to becoming a cheerleader. It is a fun and challenging sport. Making the team is just the beginning. There are many ways to grow in your skills.

Watching other squads cheer can help your team come up with new ideas.

GLOSSARY

COMMITMENT
A promise to do something.

JUNIOR VARSITY
A team whose members are younger and less experienced than members on a varsity team.

NUTRITION
Eating the right foods for health and growth.

ROUTINE
A series of movements that are repeated for a performance.

SPOTTER
A person who watches or helps a cheerleader to keep them from getting hurt.

SQUAD
A small group doing the same activity, often a physical activity.

STAMINA
Physical or mental strength that allows someone to do something for a long time.

STUNT
An exciting and sometimes dangerous move or jump during a cheer routine.

VARSITY
The most skilled team in a particular sport.

WORKSHOP
A class where people learn skills used in doing something.

FOR MORE INFORMATION

BOOKS

Gassman, Julie. *Cheerleading Really Is a Sport*. Mankato, MN: Stone Arch Books, 2011.

Leffel, Caitlin, ed. *Cheerleading: From Tryouts to Championships*. New York: Universe, 2007.

Webber, Rebecca. *Varsity's Ultimate Guide to Cheerleading*. New York: Little, 2014.

WEBSITES

To learn more about Cheerleading, visit **booklinks.abdopublishing.com**. These links are routinely monitored and updated to provide the most current information available.

INDEX

ABOUT THE AUTHOR

Marcia Amidon Lusted has written more than 100 books and 500 magazine articles for young readers on many different subjects from animals to countries to rock groups. She is also an editor and a musician. She lives in New England.